To Parents and Teachers:

We hope you and the children will enjoy reading this story in English and French. It is simply told, but not *simplified,* so that both versions are quite natural. However, there is lots of repetition for practicing pronunciation, for helping develop memory skills, and for reinforcing comprehension.

At the back of the book, there is a simple picture dictionary with key words as well as a basic pronunciation guide to the whole story.

Here are a few suggestions for using the book:

- First, read the story aloud in English to become familiar with it. Treat it like any other picture book. Look at the drawings, talk about the story, the characters, and so on.

- Then look at the picture dictionary and repeat the key words in French. Make this an active exercise. Ask the children to say the words out loud instead of reading them.

- Go back and read the story again, this time in English and French. Don't worry if your pronunciation isn't quite correct. Just have fun trying it out. If necessary, check the guide at the back of the book, but you'll soon pick up how to say the French words.

- When you think you and the children are ready, try reading the story in French only. Ask the children to say it with you. Only ask them to read it if they seem eager to try. The spelling could be confusing and discourage them.

- Above all, encourage the children, and give them lots of praise. They are usually quite unselfconscious, so let them be children and playact, try different voices, and have fun. This is an excellent way to build confidence for acquiring foreign language skills.

First paperback edition for the United States, its Dependencies, Canada, and the Philippines published 2000 by Barron's Educational Series, Inc. Text © Copyright 1998 by b small publishing, Surrey, England.

International Standard Book Number 0-7641-1389-5   Library of Congress Catalog Card Number 99-76382
Printed in Hong Kong   9 8 7 6 5 4 3 2 1

Get dressed, Robbie

Habille-toi, Robbie

Lone Morton

Pictures by Anna C. Leplar
French by Christophe Dillinger

BARRON'S

Every morning, Robbie's mom lays out clothes for him to get dressed.

Chaque matin, la maman de Robbie lui prépare des habits pour qu'il s'habille.

But some mornings Robbie likes to choose his own clothes.

Mais certains matins, Robbie préfère choisir ses habits tout seul.

Sometimes Robbie puts on clothes
that are too big,

Parfois Robbie met des habits qui
sont trop grands,

and sometimes clothes that
are too small.

et parfois des habits qui
sont trop petits.

Sometimes Robbie puts on winter clothes,

Parfois Robbie met des habits d'hiver,

and sometimes summer clothes.

et parfois des habits d'été.

And sometimes he puts on clothes from his dressing-up box!

Et parfois il choisit des habits dans sa malle à déguisements!

But today, Robbie puts on his green, spotty T-shirt,

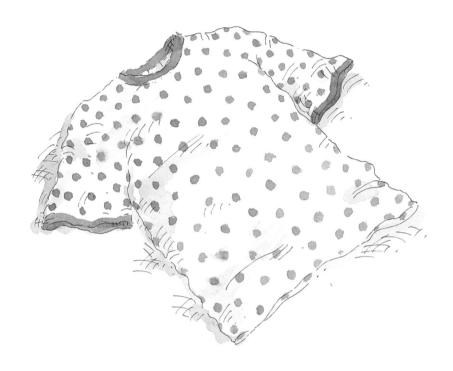

Mais aujourd'hui, Robbie choisit son T-shirt vert à pois,

his patterned shorts,

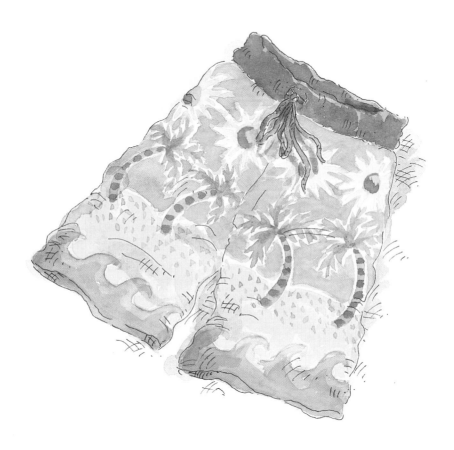

son short à motifs,

one orange sock,
une chaussette orange,

one striped sock,
une chaussette à rayures,

one blue plastic sandal,
une sandale en plastique bleu,

one crocodile slipper,
un chausson en forme de crocodile,

his pink baseball cap,
sa casquette de baseball rose,

a very long, checked scarf,
une très longue écharpe à carreaux,

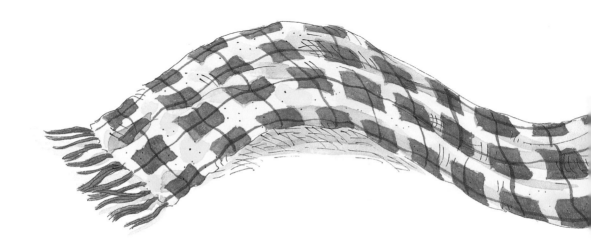

a pair of sunglasses,
une paire de lunettes de soleil,

a necklace of wooden beads,
un collier de boules en bois,

and his brand-new backpack, with his favorite car and ten color crayons.

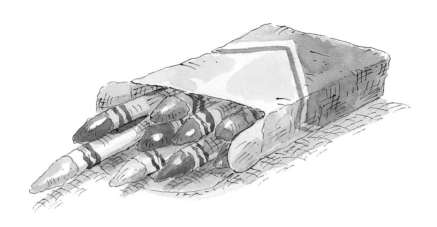

et son sac à dos tout neuf avec sa voiture préférée et dix crayons de couleur.

"Robbie, we have to go out!"
calls Mom. "Are you dressed yet?"

"Robbie, il est l'heure de sortir!"
crie maman. "Es-tu enfin habillé?"

"Yes," says Robbie, "I am dressed.

I'm going to wear this...!"

"Oui," dit Robbie. "Je suis habillé.

Je vais mettre ça...!"

Pronouncing French

Don't worry if your pronunciation isn't quite correct. The important thing is to be willing to try. The pronunciation guide here will help but it cannot be completely accurate:

- Read the guide as naturally as possible, as if it were English.
- Put stress on the letters in *italics,* e.g. show-*set*.
- Don't roll the r at the end of the word, for example, in the French word **le** (the): ler.

If you can, ask a French-speaking person to help and move on as soon as possible to speaking the words without the guide.

Note: French adjectives usually have two forms, one for masculine and one for feminine nouns. They often look very similar but are pronounced slightly differently, e.g. **petit** and **petite** (see below).

Words Les Mots
leh moh

clothes
les habits
lez *abee*

T-shirt
le T-shirt
ler tee-*shirt*

big
grand/grande
groh/grond

small
petit/petite
p'*tee*/p'*teet*

shorts

le short

ler short

backpack

le sac à dos

ler sak ah *doh*

sandals

les sandales

leh son*dal*

scarf

l'écharpe

leh*sharp*

slipper

le chausson

ler showss-*oh*

sunglasses

les lunettes de soleil

leh loo*net* der sol*ay*

socks

les chaussettes

leh show-*set*

car

la voiture

lah vwat-*yoor*

green
vert/verte

vair/vairt

orange
orange

o-ronsh

blue
bleu/bleue

bl'/bl'

pink
rose

roz

crayons
les crayons

leh crayoh

necklace
le collier

ler colee-eh

winter
l'hiver

leevair

cap
la casquette

la kasket

summer
l'été

let-ay

striped
à rayures

ah ray-oor

spotty
à pois

ah pwah

checked
à carreaux

ah karoh

patterned
à motifs

ah moteef

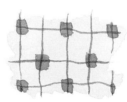

A simple guide to pronouncing this French story

Habille-toi, Robbie
a*bee* twah, ro*bee*

Chaque matin, la maman de Robbie lui prépare des habits
shack ma*tah*, la mam*oh* de ro*bee* lwee preh-*pah* deza*bee*

pour qu'il s'habille.
poor keel sa*bee*

Mais certains matins, Robbie préfère choisir ses habits tout seul.
meh sair*tah* mat*ah*, ro*bee* preh-*fair* shwah-*zeer* seza*bee* too sirl

Parfois Robbie met des habits qui sont trop grands,
pah-*fwah* ro*bee* meh deza*bee* kee soh troh grohn

et parfois des habits qui sont trop petits.
eh pah-*fwah* deza*bee* kee soh troh p'*tee*

Parfois Robbie met des habits d'hiver,
pah-*fwah* ro*bee* meh deza*bee* dee*vair*

et parfois des habits d'été.
eh pah-*fwah* deza*bee* det-*ay*

Et parfois il choisit des habits dans sa malle à déguisements!
eh pah-*fwah* eel shwa*zee* deza*bee* doh sah mal ah deh-geez-*moh*

Mais aujourd'hui, Robbie choisit son T-shirt vert à pois,
meh o'shoor-*dwee*, robee shwa*zee* soh tee-*shirt* vair ah pwah

son short à motifs,
soh short ah mo*teef*

une chaussette orange,
oon show-*set* o-*ronsh*

une chaussette à rayures,
oon show-*set* ah ray-*oor*

une sandale en plastique bleu,
oon son*dal* ohn plas*teek* bl'

un chausson en forme de crocodile,
ahn showss-*oh* ohn form der croko*deel*

sa casquette de baseball rose,
sah kas-*ket* der base*boll* roz

une très longue écharpe à carreaux,
oon treh longer eh*sharp* ah ka*roh*

une paire de lunettes de soleil,
oon pair der loo*net* der sol*ay*

un collier de boules en bois,
ahn colee-*yeh* der bool ohn bwah

et son sac à dos tout neuf avec sa voiture préférée et dix crayons de couleur.
eh soh sak ah doh too nerf avek sa vwat-*yoor* prefair*ay* et dee cray*oh* der cool*er*

"Robbie, il est l'heure de sortir!" crie maman. "Es-tu enfin habillé?"
ro*bee*, eel eh lur der sor*teer*, cree ma*moh*, eh too oh*fah* abee*yeh*

"Oui," dit Robbie. "Je suis habillé. Je vais mettre ça…!"
wee, dee ro*bee*, sh' swee abee*yeh*, sh' veh mair-tr' sah